Then I Worship

Janice Neeley

THANK YOU LADIES!

I take this opportunity to give thanks to some amazing, virtuous and powerful women of God who have been and continue to be outstanding role models in my life. My great grandmother Matilda, who exemplified love beyond measure, her home was always extended to our neighborhood, and her Sunday dinners were beyond compare to others. Apples didn't fall from the tree, my grandmother Dollie (Jay), was somewhat quiet but amazingly relevant, she knew how to provide a feast in the middle of a famine, God gave her the wit and physical ability to farm any land that He provided for her. She didn't own acres of land, but she knew how to make every house a home, not only for her family but on many occasions, she shared her home for shelter to many who were homeless from time to time.

I believe God blessed me to have the best mother (Marie) in this life, despite all of her life's challenges, she is a great woman of strength and resilience, thank you mother for loving the unloveable. My aunt Johnnie Mae demonstrated to me the ability to avoid negative confrontation and she protected me by any means necessary.

I thank God for my daughter (Tiffany), who is an awesome, strong-willed lady of God, an amazing mother to my grandchildren, she keeps me grounded and is evident that God is her Peace. Last but certainly not least, I appreciate God for my pastor...Pastor Dionne Bivins, she has truly been an asset to my spiritual and natural life, her faith in God and her loyalty to Him, has caused me to always expect nothing but the best from God, thank you Pastor Dee for believing in me. Thanks to everyone who supports my God-Given Vision, you play a vital role in the success of "Then I Worship".

CONTENTS

ACKNOWLEDGMENTS i

Introduction iii

The Inevitable 1

Our Demise 4

My Truth 17

God's Word Revealed 26

Then I Worship 39

My Motto...60

The Legacy Lives On 61

Synopsis of "Then I Worship" 62

About the Author...................................63

ACKNOWLEDGMENTS

I give thanks and homage to you God, from whom all blessings flow. You are totally responsible for inspiring me to write this book. It is because of your unmerited Grace, Mercy and constant Love, that "Then I Worship" has been given the opportunity to surface in my life and the lives of every reader. I would have never been able to pen my truth if it weren't for your guiding hands and your Heart of Justice. I am forever GRATEFUL and will always acknowledge you for being the very cause of my JOY!!!

INTRODUCTION

My Inspiration for writing this book is to share with you my truth and transparency of the challenges that I struggled with while bereaving the loss of my son. I had to endure many challenges in my lifestyle that eventually impacted me spiritually, mentally and physically.

Transparency is defined in the Cambridge English Dictionary as "the quality of being easy to see through." I want you to have a vivid picture in your mind of the challenges that my family and I had to endure during our time of bereavement. My prayer is for you to understand that every human being will process or cope with their loss in their own unique way. I use the word "unique" because God with His infinite wisdom has created each of us "fearfully and wonderfully," (Psalm 139:14 KJV) and all of us possess many different emotions that are often manifested in our time of bereavement. My hope is that you will find comfort, encouragement and strength while you read and understand my story as each chapter unfolds.

One of the most amazing lessons that I've learned during my bereavement experience, is that no one else can instruct me or anyone else on how to cope with the loss of a loved one. Most people mean well and for the most part it is good to lend an ear and appreciate what they have to say, but if their conversation begins with "If I were you I would do this, that and the other," it may be a wise decision to separate yourself from that negative energy and find comfort, wisdom, knowledge and understanding from someone who will share with you the truth and the truth of God's word. As it is written by the Psalmist David, (Psalm 1:1 KJV), "Blessed is the man that walks not in the counsel of the ungodly." A bereavement experience isn't a time to compare yourself to others because no one can be more you than you, and as God strengthens you through His word, you too will become a testimony to share with others who will encounter such loss.

As we gain knowledge and understanding of God's will for our lives through our struggles, we, ourselves should cease from criticism and judgement of others as well. There are tremendous mental struggles that will attack the bereaved and instead of judging them, we should utilize our time by praying for them, showing and giving love to them and what I believe is so much more important and helpful is to give the bereaved time and space to process the effects of their loss. It is during these times that God's hand of Mercy, Grace, Love and His Will for their lives will be manifested.

THE INEVITABLE

Death is defined in Merriam-Webster's Dictionary as "The end of life, the time ends when someone or something dies."

For every God given life to man, woman, boy, and girl, it is inevitable that death will knock at our door and we will have no other choice but to answer. Whether by life threatening illnesses, fatal accidents, or natural causes, no God given spiritual being will be able to cheat death nor escape it, all of us will have to succumb to it by giving up this present/natural life as we know it. The wise man Solomon sums death's reality in a nut shell; in the book of Ecclesiastes chapter 3:1-2/KJV, he writes; "to everything there is a season, and a time to every purpose under the heaven: A time to be born and a time to die."

When death happens, it carries with it a weight that is tremendously heavy and it is humanly impossible for any individual to carry alone. God is the only one that I know who is able to carry all of our heavy burdens and provide healing to our troubled minds, mending to our broken hearts and strength to our frail, weak bodies. God instructs us in 1st Peter 5:7(NKJV) that we can "cast all our cares upon Him for He cares for us."

In one of Elizabeth Kubler Ross' book On Death and Dying, she discussed five different stages of death that many individuals will experience during their time of bereavement:

1. Anger
2. Denial
3. Bargaining
4. Depression
5. Acceptance

Depending on the circumstances involving the cause of death, at any given moment you will experience one of the above said emotions and I don't believe that there is a time limit on how long each stage will endure. However, in making that statement, I want you to understand that you are not alone, God is ever present with you and He is well able to provide you, your family and friends with His "Peace that surpasses all understanding." (Philippians 4:7 NKJV).

The subject of death isn't one that will cause families or individuals to sit around the dinner table and have a candid discussion about. I believe that the number one reason for this non-verbal conversation is the very fact that death is a finality of truth, it is irreversible, our natural body will "go back to the earth/dust from which it was made and the Spirit shall return unto God who gave it," (Ecclesiastes 12:7 KJV). Regardless of how much our hearts ache, how many tears our eyes will cry or

how often we ask God WHY, natural life is over,
death has stamped: IT IS FINISHED!

OUR DEMISE

On Saturday night August 23, 2003, the lives of our family members changed suddenly and drastically. My husband and I tragically lost our only son, and our daughter, Tiffany, lost her only brother in a motor vehicle accident. As much as I would like to forget that period of time in my life, I can still remember the events that happened like it was only yesterday.

Prior to receiving such tragic news, I was doing what I would normally do in preparing or making things ready for church the following Sunday. God's word reveals to us in Proverbs 16:9/NKJV, "A man's heart plans his way, But the Lord directs his steps." I followed the same routine that I'd been doing for a number of years, but instead of preparing Sunday dinner that Saturday night, I was preparing nacho cheese dip to take to church to have for sale for the Usher Board Department. I chose my Sunday wardrobe apparel, shoes, accessories, etc., and while I was making things ready for myself, our son Herman Jr., AKA, "P" had finished taking his shower and as he was getting dressed, he informed that he and some of his friends were going out for a while. He would first go and give some money to Sharon, his daughter Brooklynn's mother. Brooklynn was only three months old at the time, and I was grateful that he was making effort to provide and spend time with his daughter, I said okay, be careful and I'll see you later...but I didn't know at the time that later really meant later.

After seeing him out, I locked our apartment door and proceeded upstairs and I began to pray. Praying before I go to bed, while I'm in bed or even getting up in the middle of the night is a necessary requirement for me, having communion with God always solidifies the inner peace that I need and it is my validation that I have someone who not only hears me but He also listens to me. I prayed not only for my son but for his friends and others as well, that God would watch over and protect them. I don't specifically always know who or what to pray for, but as it is written in God's word in Romans 8:26/NIV, "In the same way, the Spirit helps us in our weakness. We don't know what we ought to pray for, but the Spirit himself intercedes for us through wordless groans," therefore I have no other choice but to comply with His word. One of the most important revelations I can share with you is the POWER of PRAYER, it can travel places that you and I may never be physically able to go. When we pray to the Most High God, Our Father in Jesus' name, He hears us and will respond to our prayer, He is the only ONE who is Omnipresent, He is everywhere at the same time and is with you and I all of the time.

As I reclined in my bed and just before drifting off to sleep, I had a feeling of concern for my son, as any parent or loved one would have for a teenaged child who has left home to go out and "kick it" with his peers. I didn't experience a gut wrenching feeling of negativity such as death, nothing that tragic entered my mind nor did God give me a sense of discernment about his death. I, however, do believe that God in His creative genius places a sense of discernment in mothers which will let us know when things aren't "just right" with our children, it may manifest itself as an out of the ordinary feeling or sometimes it may be given in a vision or in a dream.

Just a little while before midnight, a Hoover police officer and a Jefferson County coroner came and knocked on our apartment door where my son and I were living at the time. Hearing an unexpected knock on your door at that time of night can immediately put a parent's mind in a state of anxiousness, a knock that no mother or loved one wants or desires to hear, a knock of discouragement, despair, and unease, a knock that will crush your heart into a million pieces and trample upon every dream of possibilities and hope that a parent or loved one has for their child, relative or friend.

I immediately got up out of bed, I felt somewhat in a daze but awake enough to first of all go and look out of my bedroom window, I noticed that it was really quite that night, but I can remember so vividly hearing birds singing... in all of my adult life I can't recall hearing birds sing like they sung that night and the best description that I can give is that it sounded tranquil to me. I know most of you have probably heard the saying "there is always a calm before a storm," and as ironic as it may sound, I believe the birds ministered to my spirit to bring a sense of peace just before I received the gut wrenching news about our son.

As I continued to look out over the parking lot, there were many cars parked that night but for some unknown reason, I had tunnel vision and the only car that I remember seeing was the Hoover police car. My first thought was "that boy has gotten himself put in jail again," and at that very thought I could feel my heart beginning to beat fast and forcefully. As I proceeded to go down stairs, each step was accompanied with uncertainty and the unknown, it wasn't a voluntary step but rather a step of involuntary.

Before I opened the door, my gut instinct feared that something was terribly wrong, and then I felt like I was moving in slow motion. Before opening the door I asked who was there, the Jefferson County coroner said his name and the Hoover police officer's name, but I can't remember their names unless I look at my son's death certificate or other demographics that has been attached to his fatal injury, and unto this very day it is still painful for me to review those documents. The coroner asked me if he could come in, I allowed him to do so but the police officer stood on the inside near the door of our apartment. The information that followed after their introduction was the beginning of the most challenging turn of events in my life and the lives of my family.

The news that the coroner delivered to me is still etched in my memory. His statement began with "ma'am, I'm sorry to say, I'm here to inform you that I believe your son has been fatally injured in a motor vehicle accident. I have his driver's license with your address on it and photos that I need you to look at to identify and verify him as your son." I couldn't believe what I was hearing, for a second or two I became confused about the profound statement, "your son has been fatally injured in a motor vehicle accident", the word fatally didn't quite register as strongly as the word injured, because what I thought I needed to hear and what I wanted to hear at that time was "your son has been injured in a motor vehicle accident with a chance of recovery," that is how I processed it in my mind but sadly enough that wasn't the case.

Hearing those words used in the same sentence were so painful and powerful, and the best way that I can describe the pain... is like having a blunt force object traumatize any part of your body that will result in severe pain. My heart began to feel like it had been stabbed with a knife and it was bleeding uncontrollably with sadness. I felt lifeless, so very weak and my mind was left in a mode of disbelief, despair and uncertainty. My upper abdomen burned with anxiety, my head was pounding so hard that it felt like my blood pressure had reached its maximum capacity of exploding.

The coroner's conversation didn't stop there, he also required of me to identify, to establish, prove to him from a photo picture I.D., that the young man who was lying lifeless on a "cooling board" was truly my son... now that request wasn't an easy process. Can you just imagine or maybe you have already had to experience how heart breaking it can be to verify to someone else that the body of the deceased, is truly your son, daughter, mother, father or friend. Well, it wasn't "just my imagination running away with me," it was my reality.

My hands were shaking nervously, my palms were sweating, my eyes were filled with tears, and for whatever reason unbeknownst to me I was unable to make a crying sound. My heart was beating with a strong force of adrenaline that I couldn't control, but I didn't break down and lose a sense of control so to speak, because honestly I didn't know what to say, how to say it, nor did I know how to respond to such tragic news. I say this with no reflection on those of you who have your own "unique" way of displaying your emotion when hearing about your loss, but at that point and without realizing it, all I could do at that moment in time was to rely the Strength and the Omniscient Power of God, and the very fact that He knew what my heart was feeling.

God has declared in His word as noted in 2nd Corinthians 12:9 NKJV, "My Grace is sufficient for you, for my power is made perfect in weakness." God's will for my life was unfolding but I was experiencing so much heartache that I couldn't recognize it. During those moments, which felt like an eternity, I had to totally depend on God to be my very source of peace. I don't consider myself to be more spiritual, more "holier than thou" or stronger than anyone else, but that of which I know about

God and His ability to give me peace in the midst of my storm is a testimony of my personal relationship that I have with Him.

As I looked at my son in the photos that the coroner presented to me, he was lying on a stretcher and he looked as if he was only asleep, I didn't see any physical or noticeable injuries to his body. The shirt and shorts he was wearing appeared to be as spotless as they were when he left home, however, when his clothes were returned to me, it was evident because of the blood stains in them that he had suffered some lacerations or trauma to some areas of his body, and as painful as it was for me to wash his clothes, I needed to protect the quality of them so that I could pass them on to his nephews, (Money-G and Guy-Rock). I truly thank God blinding my eyes for that period of time, and preserving our son's body in such a way that he didn't appeared to have suffered any more physical trauma than he actually had.

I felt lifeless, my body felt numb all over and every thought and communication that I had with the coroner somewhat reminded me of having a nightmare that would not come to closure. I heard what he was saying but I didn't hear with my ears but rather with my heart. It was such an unreal but so real moment, my mind couldn't or I didn't allow it to grasp the reality that our son, Herman Jr. was dead. I was in my period of denial, even though the evidential facts were there, I denied the reality in my mind.

How should a parent or loved one feel or react when losing their child, loved one, or friend? Is there a protocol that we are to adhere to when we are faced with such tragic news? I know that most of you have heard the cliché, "children should bury their parents not parents bury their children." Never in a million years did my husband and I think or even imagine that our family would have to prepare ourselves for the burial of either of our children. The New International Bible records in Psalm 139:16, "Your eyes saw my unformed body; all the days ordained for me were written in your book before one of them came to be." God is the only one who knows the beginning, middle and the ending of our days on this earth, however, understanding that and accepting that reality, is a battle in the mind of the bereaved.

After I verbally identified to the coroner that the young man in the photos was my son, he informed me of the procedures that our family would have to initiate, once we were done with the formality of releasing Herman Jr.'s body, he would then be picked up and transferred to the funeral home of our choice. After receiving all of the instruction from the coroner, he and the police officer offered their condolences and they exited our apartment. Still in a moment of disbelief, I went upstairs and called my daughter and son-in-law at the time and informed them of Herman Jr.'s death, they along with my grandchildren came to our apartment and I shared with them the incident to the best of my ability and there wasn't a dry eye in the house, that period of time for us was life changing to say the least.

I felt somewhat like Job in the bible did, when

God allowed Satan to attack him, Job lost everything that he had and all of his children. The Lord gave Satan permission to attack Job to prove to him that he wasn't just serving Him for things. The bible says that Job was "perfect, upright and he feared God." One thing that the Lord didn't allow Satan to do, and that was to touch Job's spirit/the man himself, the magnet that connected him with the Lord. Satan caused boils to attack his body, his sons were killed by a windstorm, his servants killed with the sword, cattle and livestock burned in the fire, and in addition to all of Job's tragedies, his wife, the one whom the Lord God had given to him to be his "help meet" asked him, "Are you still holding firmly to your integrity, curse God and die" (Job 2:9 NET). Our family didn't lose or suffer half as much as Job did, but when I read about the testing of his faith, I know that he experienced and felt a tremendous amount of heartache, disappointment, pain and sorrow. According to the word of the Lord in Job 3:1, Job cursed the very day that he was born, that was evident to me that the suffering that he had to endure took a toll on him both mentally and physically.

For the next several days our family went forth in making funeral arrangements, we experienced a tremendous amount of emotional and mental distress, we had to come together and follow a painful protocol of putting Herman Jr. to rest. If dying along was the end of the story, then just maybe our hearts wouldn't have to ache as much, but when we are forced to proceed with making preparation to bury a loved one, nothing about it feels right, each process is a constant reminder that their nature existence is over for them, never to be present again in this life.

From the very moment that we entered into the Funeral Home, it brought about a nerve wracking sense of obligation, but it was necessary for our family to give Herman Jr. a proper burial. Our first encounter was the viewing of his body, which was covered in a white sheet-type cloth or material, he was covered from his chest down to his feet. As we stood and looked upon him, we were all in a state of agony, none of us were able to hold back the tears and our verbal communication ceased. Some of us held each other's hand while others embraced one another. As his mother, I wanted so much to take my baby in my arms and hold him and never let go, but because of the funeral home's protocol I could only rub his head and his hair, which was a different and difficult experience for me. Because of the preservation of his body and the fact that the blood line of life had been severed, the very hairs on his head felt ice cold and it sent chills throughout my entire body.

After the viewing of his body, we went to the funeral home director's office, there he showed us a catalog of caskets from which we had to choose to have Herman Jr.'s body housed and buried in, that process didn't feel any better, we all felt like we were going from bad to worse, and in all actuality we were. As I turned the pages of the catalog one after another, I could feel my head well up with more tears, I completely lose my composure, I was still teary-eyed because of the viewing of Herman Jr.'s body, and then we had to pick and choose a casket to house his body for burial and all I could do was weep which increased with intensity.

I began manifesting my stage of anger, I was so angry because of the entire process that we had to go through and I had a lot of questions in my head that I needed and wanted answers to, but had none, one of which was, WHY? Why did God allow this to happen to our family at this time in our lives, our son was much too young to die. I cried out to my family and verbalized to them, "I CAN'T DO THIS, I DON'T WANT TO DO THIS! They responded to my cry in an amazing way... despite the fact that they were experiencing a tremendous amount of pain as well, they were present with me through the entire process, encouraging me, loving on me, and for that I am so grateful to God, for my family, friends, and I am especially thankful for my children's father, Herman Sr., even with his heartache, he supported me and our daughter with his love every step of the way. I believe he realized and I know that when we lose someone to death or when relationships have been severed, it is not the time to find fault or blame and bicker back and forth with the other person, because it doesn't and won't change the present reality. There must be a level of adulthood that should persevere in unity.

After we finished looking through most of the catalog of caskets, we were shown some of the caskets that were on display at the funeral home as well, we looked at several different styles and colors and we decided on a nice, steel blue colored casket, which was one of Herman Jr.'s favorite colors...

after all he was a "Spain Park Jaguar." Was that an easy process? No, not by any means but it was necessary, we chose an emblem of the Praying Hands which was displayed on the interior panel of the inside lid of his casket. Our selection of the Praying Hands emblem was a commemorative gesture...shortly after Herman Jr. turned eighteen years old, he took it upon himself to get a tattoo on his upper right arm, and yes you guessed correctly, it was the Praying Hands emblem, I'm sure he had many other emblems to choose from, but he chose the one that was significant to him. Prayer is an important virtue for our family, it is our way of communing with God and it has always been a significant foundation for us. As far back as I can remember, from my great grandma Mitilda, grandmother, Jay and my mother Marie, prayer has always been and will continue to be a vital element that will bind our family together. It was an essential element that we needed to help us get through our grieving process, I'm grateful to everyone who were a part of our circle, the need to pray never ceased.

One important thing that I have learned about losing a loved one or even when a friendship has been severed, is that life doesn't lie dormant, don't get me wrong and please understand that I am grateful to God for each Graced given day that He affords me, but it is life's circumstances that forces us to re-route our point of interest in another direction. Pressing through the pain sometimes seems endless, but because God lives, He causes all the pieces of the puzzle to fit perfectly together, because His Grace and Mercy abounds we have Hope that never fails.

MY TRUTH

After Herman Jr.'s funeral, everyone went their own separate ways, life started back up as usual, but for our family and friends life as usual felt like we had taken a detour to a life of unusual. The strength in numbers that we had previously shared with one another began to dwindle down as we advanced further in each of our own individual lives. Life caused us to gradually distance ourselves from one another, not only physically but verbally as well, we didn't call and check on one another as much. I wasn't really disappointed about not receiving as many calls or initiating them as I had been previously, because I understood that we all had our own lives to resume and there was still the challenge of having to cope with the loss of our son, our brother and our friend.

As life fast forwarded several months into our bereavement, some of our family and friends seem to have found comfort in talking about how it used to be when Herman Jr. was alive, others may have avoided talking about him all together. I was one of those who chose not to talk about him as much, I felt like I wanted so much more than having a mere conversation about how it used to be when he was alive. I longed to have a face to face encounter with him, something tangible, I desired to hear him laugh, hear myself fuss at him when he didn't clean up his room or when he broke curfew, and at the same time I would be in our kitchen preparing food for him to eat.

There were many times when someone else would bring up a conversation about him, and out of courtesy to them, I would involve myself in the conversation but I didn't allow it to consume me to the point that it would cause them to think that it was okay, and that I was ready to move on past my grieving process, because honestly I wasn't quite there yet. I felt like I was in a strange land and my place of normalcy was being challenged and I really didn't know how to respond to it.

Sharing my truth of how I coped with the loss of our son will probably shock most of you who are reading this book, but for others it will give you a sense of confirmatory gratitude for hearing such truth, it will validate for you similar challenges of what you have experienced as you were going through your loss as well. Please remember friends, each and every one of us will cope with our loss in various, different ways, but what's more important is to know that we have "The High Priest" who knows what we are going through and "He can be touched by the feeling of our infirmities, He too was tempted just as we are but without sin." (Hebrews 4:15KJV).

I knew that God wasn't the author of confusion and

I had His Spirit on the inside of me, but for a long period of time I couldn't or I didn't desire to break that negative cycle of anger and frustration. I had a choice to think on positive things but more often than none, my thoughts were pretty negative and filled with gloom, doom and despair. Our son's death left me thinking that it wasn't necessary for me to continue living, and I asked God on many occasions, WHY did this happen to our family at such a time as it did? Herman Jr. was too young to die so soon.

There were times when I thought about some of his friends who were still alive, I would compare and contrast the difference between our son's attitudes and attributes to those of his friends, some good and some not so good, and in my mind it didn't quite add up the way I thought it should have. I didn't understand why our son had to answer death's call and some of his friends were still alive, no negative reflections on his friends or their families but that was my way of processing, reasoning or bargaining, which had me totally confused, broken and left without answer, maybe the answers were there, I just simply refused to accept them.

My husband and I only had two children, our daughter Tiffany who was twenty six years old and Herman Jr. was eighteen years old. Before his death I believe they were just getting to a point in their lives when they were beginning to have their sister/brother talks or conversations, there were times when they would disagree, fuss, fight and fall out with one another, but because of their relationship which was bonded by love, it would eventually force them to make up or make it right. But after we lost him, the reality of it all ceased for her, she was my oldest child but she was still my baby girl and my heart ached for her. For so many days I felt like I had cheated our daughter out of the ability to share laughter and sibling rivalry with her brother, because of the decision that her dad and I had made not to have any more children; a lot of guilt about a lot of things will manifest itself when death is relevant.

My thought pattern didn't line up with the things that God told me in His word to think on, (Philippians 4:8), instead of thinking on things that were true, just and honest, I thought just the opposite. I entertained the thought of suicide on many occasions, but I thank God for His revealed word, as noted in 1st Corinthians 6:19-20, it basically states that "my body is the temple of the Holy Ghost which is inside of me, which belongs to God, I have been bought with a price," the blood shed of Jesus Christ, and with that truth I understood that I was a bereaved mother but not the devil's fool, (unwise). I believe if I had committed suicide, it would have only granted me eternal damnation, and seriously who has time for that, therefore, I resolved with the truth that God is the giver of life and when it's my time to answer death's call, it will be as a result of God withdrawing His spirit from me.

I don't apologize for speaking my truth, it is liberating for me to be able to stand naked (not literally) before God, out of an earnest heart with a broken and contrite spirit, and share with you my brokenness and how I received my puncture wounds and battle scars. My desire is to encourage each of you make you aware that it was God and Only God who Loved me through my pain and has given me a sense of peace in the midst of my anguish. I knew within my heart that God would strengthen me and bring me to a place of consolation, but I didn't know how and I didn't know when that season of manifestation would occur.

As God graced me with more days, more months and years, the more the devil would intensify his deception of negativity. John 10:10 says that, "the thief comes only to steal and kill and destroy," and he really had a heyday in my mind. I felt like I just didn't want to go on, a spirit of depression began to overwhelm me, simply getting out of bed was a major task for me, because it validated the truth that I had to realize, and that was, our son was dead and there wasn't a thing in this world that me or my family could do about it. I wasn't receptive to such truth, and it left me physically weak and I refused to fight back with the devil. But God who has all power, picked me up and carried me through some of the most difficult times in my life. When I was at my lowest level of hopelessness, He was always present, in spite of me/the woman in the mirror, His Love never failed.

.

Several years prior to losing our son, my children's father and I were having some significant challenges in our marriage that eventually caused us to drift apart spiritually, mentally, physically and financially. I was at my "wit's end," and after much prayer and Godly counsel, I was faced with the challenge of having to make a really tough decision, one of which would change our lives tremendously. I shared with my family, my daughter and my son-in-law at the time, some of the challenges that we were having, I tried to be as discreet as possible because I didn't want to become a burden to them nor did I want my husband to reap any negative feedback from my family. I appreciate my family for not only listening to what I had to say but more importantly they didn't force their opinions upon me, they allowed me to make my own decision and they loved me enough to share their home and provided financial assistance when we needed it.

My children's father and I weren't a couple who really knew how to verbally communicate with one another, which is so very important in any relationship. Most of the time the communication that we shared was in an argumentative form, which left me with a spirit of fear which is torment. That being said, I really didn't know how I was going to inform my husband of my decision to leave our home, because I knew he would not receive that information in a humbled position, but I knew it had to be done. I was totally fatigued and I didn't have the strength to fight anymore, I just wanted to leave and start afresh somewhere else other than where I was. I don't know if you would consider what I'm about to say was my "ram in the bush" or not, but as a result of what happen, I felt better about my decision to leave.

One morning when my children's father wasn't

present in the home for whatever the reason was at the time, I informed our son that we were leaving our present home to go and stay with his sister and brother-in-law for a while. I didn't go into any details, but because he had witness some of the challenges I was faced with, I believe he understood that I had his best interest at heart. We started grabbing and packing some of our belongings and putting them in our car, I wasn't concerned about taking any more than our basic necessities/clothes and shoes. As we were hurriedly moving items out of the house and into the car, my thoughts were that we would be gone before his father made it home and I wouldn't have to tell him of our departure face to face, but it didn't quite pan out that way.

While in the house, I made a conscious effort to look out of the window to see if his father was coming home, and after a while I saw him getting out of a car, a mode of transportation that wasn't his own and that is all I'll say about that. He entered the house and saw us packing and asked what was going on, I explained to him that we were leaving, and OMG!, one word lead to another, he was livid and I was pretty heated myself. I was nervous and angry all at the same time but I didn't back down because I knew that my heart had left our home even before I decided to physically depart. I continued to move a few more of our things out of the house and I realized that our son had witnessed yet another argument, the last load of our belongings that I made it out of the house with was truly the last one, it was then that I made the decision not to go back into the house for any more of our things. Even though I was angry and nervous about leaving our home and the fear of the unknown, the Spirit of God rushed in and gave me much needed peace in my mind about making the decision to leave when I did. I never looked back, my decision to leave forced me to walk by Faith and it taught me to NEVER allow another human being or any negative situation that I may encounter, to hold me hostage in fear ever again!

For so long I would mentally beat myself up with guilt because my thoughts were, if I had only stayed in our home and endured the challenges for a little while longer, maybe our marriage would have taken a turn for the better, and if that had been the case, then just maybe our son would be alive today. I had a lot of "what if" scenarios that played out in my head, what if I had been a better wife and mother, a better listener, provider, what if I had engaged more in learning how to communicate with my children's father. What if, what if, what if, but the truth of the matter was, it didn't and would not have change the reality that our son of eighteen years was gone, never again would we be able to hear him talk or laugh, never to share in the laughter and the tears of helping him while he was learning the art of parenting his own child.

For so many days those thoughts and questions haunted me, and it happened most of the time while I was commuting from one place to another. Have you ever been traveling and lose your train of thought or sense of direction, and you didn't remember how you got from one destination to the next? Well, that is how those thoughts would consumed me, and despite all of the negative energy that I allowed to enter my mind, God remained Faithful to me, His Angels protected me from danger that I could and could not see, His hand of Mercy and Heart of Love remained steadfast.

GOD'S WORD REVEALED

As time traveled forward and as I continued to read God's word, I was on mission to find some level of peace within my mind and spirit that would provide comfort for me while coping with the loss of our son. But so many times all I could focus on and think about was finding a word from the Lord that would benefit our son even while he laid lifeless in his grave. I know that some of you may be thinking that the above statement is somewhat unbelievable and ridiculous, and I'm okay with that because I understand that God has made all of us with different coping mechanisms.

Our daughter, Tiffany and I have had similar thoughts, that is, when we could find the strength and the courage to conversed with one another about her brother, most of the time when we would engage in a conversation about him, it would cause the both of us break down and start crying, then we would dry our eyes, talk some more and break down all over again. Our hearts were not only grieving because of his death, but we had a desire to find answers to questions that we had often wondered about. Questions such as: what were his last words, did he suffer much before God withdrew His Spirit, what kind of mental or physical state would he have been in if he had only lived? But our main concern was had he "made peace with God," where would he spend eternity beyond his final earthly resting place. My daughter and I are believers of the Gospel of Jesus Christ and we understand why Jesus laid down His life for sinners, that being said we believe that there is only one of two places in which my son or any other deceased individual will spend eternity, and that will be either heaven or hell. There isn't a human being on this earth that is wise enough to escape both places.

In the year of 2008, God began to enlighten my mind with some truths about our son's confession of Faith in Him. At the time I didn't quite know how to follow the path that He was leading me to, but I had to come to the realization that God understood my struggles and I had to simply trust and have faith in Him. He was the only one who could answer our questions about my son's hereafter. God never ceased to amaze me with revelation of His infinite wisdom, He knows when and how to reveal His truth through His word. He said in Matthew 7:7 KJV, "Ask and it shall be given to you, seek and you will find, knock and the door will be opened to you." My daughter and I could only hope that at some point in time in our lives God would answer some of our questions according to His will.

God revealed to me that because I had focused so much energy on the desire to know where my son was spending eternity, I had somehow forgotten some important facts about the path that he had guided me to and through. On June 2nd 1985, while attending church locally near our home, after the preached word went forth and the alter call was made, I answered God's call of repentance, I was baptized in Jesus' name and the Lord reconciled me back unto Himself according to my confession of faith in the death, burial and resurrection of Jesus Christ. As I was growing in Grace and in the knowledge of God, He instilled in me the ability to teach my children how to grow up in the fear (reverence) and knowledge of Him. My daughter was eight years old and Herman Jr. was four months old when I received God's Spirit.

The Lord helped me to understand that it was imperative for me to learn how to teach and train my children in the way that they should go. The wise man Solomon was a God-inspired writer, who penned words of wisdom for all parents in Proverbs 22:6/KJV, "train up a child in the way he should go: and when he is old, he will not depart from it." When our children are young, they are at the perfect age when their hearts are tender and their minds are receptive to the call of God. Jesus told His disciples in Matthew 19:14 (NLT), "Let the children come to me, don't stop them, for the Kingdom of Heaven belongs to those who are like children." For all of us who have either birth, adopted, fostered or helped raised children, we should understand that our children are not exempt from knowing who God is, and why He sent His only begotten son (Jesus) to die their sins. It is our responsibility as parents to expose, introduce and teach them of how important it is for them to get to know God for themselves, because Satan is ready and available on a daily basis to introduce himself to them.

God started walking me down memory lane, He began to rehearse some truths in my mind. It was only because of His Grace and Mercy, my faith in His word and prayers from our community of faith that in the year of 1990, our daughter Tiffany made her confession of Faith in Jesus Christ. She was baptized and received The Holy Spirit. Our hearts rejoiced with gladness because she became a by-product of the teaching that God had placed within me. And when our son, Herman Jr. was twelve years old, a year or so after we had moved in with his sister and brother-in-law, he made it known to us that he wanted to be baptized and saved. We were all somewhat taken by surprise but it sounded like music to our ears. My daughter, her husband and I were all believers in the Lord and we made great effort to live our lives pleasing to God and to manifest His goodness in the presence of our children.

As a result of Herman Jr.'s confession, I talked with him in the best possible way that I could at his age level of understanding. I made him aware of the truth that God loved him so much that He gave His only begotten son, (Jesus Christ) to die for his sins and if he believed in Jesus he would have everlasting life. And it was important for him to know as well that because of his confession, he would be rejected by many of his friends and acquaintances and there would be times when he would make some not so wise choices, but I assured him that God loved him and with His help everything would be alright. I prayed for him and he began to cry and so did I, we didn't cry because we were sad but I believe that because God knew our son's heart was in a broken and repentant state, He was in the process of preparing him for something greater. God had answered yet another prayer, the son he gave us, a sinner had repented, and the Angels in Heaven were rejoicing.

We knew that Herman Jr. didn't really understand why he wanted or needed to be baptized and saved, and who really knows and understands at the beginning of conception, but we believed that he knew that he needed God in his life and that need was manifested several years later. While attending a church service with some of his friends who witnessed that great experience, Herman Jr. was baptized and received the Gift of God's Spirit!

I was so grateful to God for renewing my son's heart, because as any mother would say, "I only want what's best for my children." God charged me with the responsibility of making sure that Herman Jr. received the foundation of His word which was necessary for him in his everyday life. I taught our son to the best of my ability of how imperative it was for him to be in constant fellowship with God, and I made every effort that I possibly could to have him in church so that he could be taught how to live his life pleasing to God. And for the most part he had no other choice but to be faithful, however, sometime prior to his sixteenth birthday he started his season of "teenage rebellion," which is typical for some teenagers, he didn't desire to attend church as much, and it became somewhat of a challenge for me to get him motivated enough to rekindle his passion for church fellowship.

I feel the need to take a sidebar now to encourage and give a round of applause to all of our mothers who are raising fatherless sons and to all of our fathers who raising motherless daughters. God has birth something special in each one of you that will result in nothing but GREATNESS! Yes, the challenges are difficult but the reward is GRAND!, you won't always say or do the right thing and you will make those parenting mistakes, but I want you to know that because God lives BIG in you, the time is NOW to hold your head up high, keep a humbled spirit and be grateful to God for counting you worthy enough to be called "momma and daddy." "Life is but a vapor that appears for a little while and then vanishes." (James 4:14 NIV).

Several month after Herman Jr.'s sixteenth birthday, he got a got a job during the summer months when he was out of school, he worked the evening/night shift most of the time, which caused him to be absent from church services at night and as a result, the more he was out of church the more he desired to stay at home, he started slacking and seemingly losing interest in going to church. On Sunday mornings I would go into his room to wake him up so that he could get ready for church, he would appear to be so tired that he sometimes wouldn't budge, he would open his eyes and acknowledge the fact that I was present, but as soon as I'd leave his room he would drift back off to sleep.

I found myself getting so angry with him at times because of his lack of interest or desire to be in church, and as a result of my frustration, I would just give up and leave him at home, I know that wasn't the right thing to do but this is my truth of how I handled the situation at the time.

I found myself trying to figure out what was going on in my son's head, I couldn't understand why he was turning away from God, the one who he needed the most in his life. As he began to adopt some lifestyle changes of "trying to find himself", he became defiant and started doing things that some of the other teenager were doing, things such as: drinking, smoking, having sex and rebelling. I'm not shifting the blame on any of the teenagers that were in his circle at the time nor am I judging that behavior because I was once a child myself and I have experienced the results of my decisions because of peer pressure. That being said, Herman Jr. made some conscious decisions or choices that were not profitable for him, but his decisions didn't stop my responsibility as a mother to love him, tell him the truth and instruct him to do the right thing. And as a result of his decisions, I believed and thought that his actions had contradicted his prior belief in God, and therefore, his relationship with God had been severed. But God, who is so merciful caused an eye opening revelation for me, believing is good in its proper setting, but it is "the truth that we know that makes us free" (John 8:32 KJV).

To give you some history of why I believed and allowed those inaccurate thoughts to occur, as I fore stated earlier, on June 2, 1985, I answered God's call of repentance and it was during those infancy years of my saved life that I became somewhat gullible to the point that I believed the information that was ministered unto me rather than studying God's word for myself. I was taught the word of God by my former pastor, who was an awesome man of God, he wasn't a novice but he was studious in the word of God.

However, the environmental setting at the time was focused more on the fact that I had to "work", I had to toil to maintain my salvation. I was ignorant/unlearned and I concluded that the pre-requisite for my continuation of Salvation, was to become a person of "I can't", I can't do this, I can't do that and if I did do something contrary to what others considered was right, I was destined for eternal damnation. And because of my lack of studying and meditating on God's word, I was always in constant fear of falling into sin and going to hell. I focused more on trying not to go to hell than I did enjoying the Beauty of my Blood-bought salvation. Please don't misconstrue what I'm saying, and I need you to have a clear understanding, that as children of the most High God there are places we shouldn't go and things we shouldn't do.

But God, whose Mercy endures forever, lead me down memory lane in His word, just as the Apostle Paul had to remind the Church at Ephesus, as penned in Ephesians 2:8-9 KJV, "For by Grace are ye saved through Faith; and that not of yourselves: it is the Gift of God. Not of works, lest any man should boast." He reminded me of the same truth about myself. A number of years after God saved me, I made some choices that were not conducive as being called a child of God, yes, I have sinned and fallen short of His Glory, I'm not proud about my choices but I am honest enough to admit it. The healing process of any problem that we encounter will begin with recognition and admission. And God who is just and Faithful, will provide us with Mercy in our time of need.

As God began to enlighten me, He ignited a spark within me that caused me to search His word for answers that could free me of the negative thoughts that I was thinking about my son's hereafter. Thoughts that didn't come from Him, but in all actuality I was the author of such confusion. I'm not shifting the blame on anyone but myself, it is one thing to think you know God's words, but it is more important to know God because of His word. When thinking is coupled with lack of knowledge, it produces ignorance/unlearned results, it's so much better to know the truth than to think you know the truth.

God, who is Omniscient and full of wisdom, revealed an "ah ha" moment to me, "HE IS NOT AN INDIAN GIVER!" He doesn't give us His Salvation and Holy Spirit based on conditions and He won't take it away from us because we sometimes fall short. Even when the children of Israel failed in obedience to the many laws that were set before them, the Lord had an action plan of atonement for them. Aaron, Moses' brother was chosen by God to be His first high priest, and whenever Israel fell short of the Glory, Aaron had to follow the instructions that the Lord had given him, he had to present unto the Lord the blood of animals for the atonement of Israel's sins. That was then and this is now, God sent Jesus Christ, Heaven's Best to be our propitiatory. He said "Think not that I am come to destroy the law or the prophets but to fulfill it" (Matthew 5:17 KJV). The Blood that flowed from the body of Jesus Christ (The Lamb of God), on the Cross at Calvary is not in vain, it was shed once and for all who believes in His death, burial and His resurrection. And with that bit of information it began to take root in my spirit and I was determined not to allow myself or the spirit of the devil to continue oppressing me with his lies of deceit.

In the month of May, the year of 2004, the Lord blessed me with my very first home, it was farther north from where I was living previously and approximately thirty-five to forty miles from my former church. I continued worshipping there for about three months until commuting that distance became somewhat of a challenge for me, mainly because of the increase in gas prices. But I knew how important it was for me to have continued communion with God, so I began visiting a local church, which was closer and the pastors and members there were of like-faith. I didn't attend their services to become a member, but rather, I was searching for the Truth of God's Word, and each time that I attended church there, God caused the pastors to deliver His word under the powerful anointing of the Holy Spirit. God's word was so powerful that it caused my spirit to soak it up like a sponge and my desire to hear God's word and to study His word increased with great intensity. As a result and with much prayer and guidance from the Lord, on August 31, 2005, I wrote a formal exit letter to my former pastor and congregation, informing them of my decision to become a member of the church that I currently attend as of today. The Lord positioned me in the right place in the right season according to His will.

Our pastors at my current church assembly have a strong and positive value system, especially when it comes to the Truth of God's word, they insist that everyone who sits under their ministry, should do so with the desire to learn and know God through His word for themselves. They live the life of integrity before God and His people and as they teach, preach and instruct us from God's word, it is our responsibility to diligently search the scriptures for ourselves, because of the simple fact that human beings are fallible and are subject to error. But God's word is forever true and will stand when everything and everybody else falls. God was still making Himself relevant in my life as I continued my studies in His word.

One bible class night, God confirmed His Salvation Plan to me again, our senior pastor began teaching out of the book of Ephesians, which is accredited to the Apostle Paul. His central message was to make sure that the Church at Ephesus understood the Truth of God's Salvation, it wasn't given to them because of what they did/their works; but rather because of the Grace and Mercy of God. My pastors, nor the congregation of my brothers and sisters were aware of the mental struggle that I was having about what I call my son's "backslidden state and the questions that I had about his salvation, but God is so AMAZING! As our senior pastor continued his teaching on the Grace and Mercy of God, I felt like shackles were falling off of my mind, the heavy load of the unknown was being lifting, and all I could do was give Praise and Honor to God. He caused His word to become alive in my spirit and my understanding of His Grace and Mercy began to unfold, it trumped all of the misconceptions that I had forced myself to believe about His Salvation for my son. For so long, I was bound with the lack of knowledge of God's Plan of Salvation, but I understand now that it is His Grace and His Mercy that will always triumph over "our need to work and toil," to gain what has already been given to us through the BLOOD OF JESUS CHRIST, HALLELUJAH!!!

God informed me that in no uncertain terms, that I was ONLY my son's mother, He allowed my family and I to have him in our lives for a set number of years. I am not my son's judge or jury and certainly not his Savior, He is a Just God and His Mercy endures forever, my son's spirit was with Him, and all I should do is totally believe in Him and His will. He guided me to His word again in Ephesians 2:8-9 KJV, "For by grace are ye saved through faith; and that not of yourselves; it is the gift of God, not of works, lest any man should boast. And God didn't stop there, He revealed to me that my son may have fallen short because of his choices but he didn't fall from His Grace and Mercy/THE BLOOD-STAINED BANNER! In 1st John 2:1 KJV is a scripture that most of us as becoming Saints don't speak much about... but just listen to what John had to say as he was inspire by The God of his day. "My dear children, these things I write unto you, that you sin not. And if any man sin, we have an advocate with the father, Jesus Christ the righteous". AMAZING GRACE!!!

One of the many things that I Love about God is that He knows how to administer His Love through conviction and not condemnation, He not only put me on the straight and narrow street concerning His Master Salvation Plan, but He broke me down to the lowest common denominator, which was non-other than me-myself. He reminded me of some sinful choices that I had not only thought upon, but also the choices I caused to manifest or put in action, and He still called me righteous, and it is all because of the Blood of Jesus Christ. He lead me into a state of humility, repentance, I had to surrender with my hands lifted high, because I know now that God didn't call or anoint me to be judge or jury over anyone. He has instructed me to Love others as Christ loved the Church and gave His life for it and He commissioned me to share The Good News of Jesus Christ, His Death, Burial and Resurrection, God's will for my life is for His Glory. So I want to encourage you, whenever you are in doubt about anything, you can always go to the source of everything, our Father God in Jesus name.

THEN I WORSHIP

After God placed me a position of acceptance of my son's final resting place and acknowledgement of His Perfect Will for my life, I started developing a devotion of not only reading His Word but I began applying His word to my everyday life's journey. After years of feeling lifeless and unmotivated, God rekindled my passion for Him, my desire to live a more abundant life became my thriving force again. I truly desired to devote myself to Him and fall in love with Him all over again.

But that passion didn't come without opposition from the devil, he started again offering me a lot of the things that my flesh desired, such as sex, alcohol and everything that accompanied it. The devil never stops, his schemes, trickery, and his lies are ever present; he was only conducting business as usual, trying to abort my God given Vision of Destiny. It has often been said, "when you take one step forward, something will happen that will knock you two steps backward," that phrase isn't scripturally based, however, the vicissitudes of life happens to every God given human being, and I certainly wasn't exempt from the weapons he was forming. But I thank God for enlightening Brother Isaiah to pen words of encouragement to us. It is found on Isaiah 54:17 KJV, "No weapon that is formed against thee shall prosper, regardless of the shape of the weapon, it will not prosper!

It was during those times of temptation that I had to learn how to PUSH and FIGHT the GOOD FIGHT of FAITH, and the BEST weapon I had to use was the WORD of God. Whenever my flesh desired what was contrary to the word of God, I had to allow my SPIRIT to grab ahold of God's word for a renewing of my mind on a daily basis. Did I always pass the test? Absolutely not, but I knew that each day and moment that God granted me with His Grace and Mercy, it afforded me the opportunity to repent and forget those things that were behind me and press forward. The apostle Paul is an amazing testimony of one who had to forget the ugliness of his past and he has left it on record for all of us to know. In the book of Philippians 3:13 KJV he writes "Brethren, I count not myself to have apprehended: but this one thing I do, forgetting those things which are behind, and reaching forth unto those things which are before." There is no way for us to successfully advance forward if we are always looking backwards.

As I began to re-fuel my spirit with God's word, He began to reveal secrets that were sacred and powerful enough to capture my attention, and it caused me to start delighting myself in Him. The word of God in the book of Psalm 37:4 KJV, encouraged me to "Delight myself in the Lord; and He will give me the desires of my heart." I have many natural desires for my life, and I believe they shall come to fruition, but my ultimate desire is to please God and fulfill my life's purpose for

Him.

The Lord wanted me to know that He is well able to cause my desires to be manifested, but it would ultimately depend on how I would respond to the process of life's tests and trials. I have to believe and know that His word is my road map and that it is filled with precise instructions for me to be victorious in every area of my life. He will only react based upon how I act through my life's challenges. I'm learning that God is a willing participant but I've got to be willing and obedient to His word and His instructions. James 2:17 KJV says, "Even so faith, if it hath not works, is dead, being alone," therefore, I have become an employer of faith and works. I trust that God is orchestrating my life and I'm allowing His word to perform and manifest itself as I read it, study it, meditate upon it and respond to it.

Wisdom and knowledge are two principle virtues that God desires for His people to obtain. James 1:5 NLT tells us, "If any of you need wisdom, ask our generous God, and He will give it to you and He will not rebuke you for asking." Now that I understand and believe how important it is to meditate and understand God's will for my life, I pray and acknowledge Him to direct my path through every circumstance or situation in my life. I read His word with great expectation to receive revelation of Him and how to apply His word, He and His word are one and they are my solid foundation. "Thy word is a lamp unto my feet and a light unto my path" (Psalm 119:105 KJV). Sure I can take any scripture in God's word and use it for my advantage; I can make the word say what I want it to say and as a result of that alteration, my flesh will be satisfied, but it will profit me nothing more except to leave me ignorant, unlearned and searching for the real truth.

For those of you who are seeking God for answers as a result of losing someone because of death or whatever the loss or situation may be, that is causing some challenges for you at this very moment and time in your life, I beseech you to seek God first, because the pain of that loss will be mind-blogging and the devil will add some of his trickery that will be harmful to your body and soul. Seeking God for guidance and direction is always "first priority" when it comes to the health of your mind, He is the one and only one who is truly concerned about you and your well-being. In the book of Isaiah 55:6 (KJV), Isaiah encouraged the Children of Israel to "Seek the Lord while He may be found, call upon Him while He is near," and I certainly concur with Isaiah, please don't deny yourself of the "Peace of God that surpasses all understanding, it shall keep your hearts and your minds in Christ Jesus" (Philippians 4:7 KJV). If you seek God first, HE is all the precedence that you will ever need. GO AHEAD AND CHECK OUT HIS TRACK RECORD/HIS HOLY WORD!!!

A prime example of one who would seek God and call upon Him when he needed Him most was King David. Most of us will identify David not because of his broken and repented heart or the very fact that God chose him as a man after His own heart, but more often than none, we will remember David's history as it relates to his sinful choices of committing adultery, which is what some of us consider to be more sinful than others, and it certainly didn't help the fact that he was also a murderer. Now, we all have the choice to think and remember what we choose, however, sometimes those privileges will cloud our minds about the genuine truth; which is at the end of the day the negative things that we remember most about people are only a part of their past, and if we allow our thoughts to condemn others, we must have a clear understanding that we have a past as well, and it will cause us to forfeit a clear vision of our future with God. He hasn't chosen us because of our sin-birth, or for the sins that we commit, He chose us in spite of our sinful nature, and He loves unconditionally; we are BLOOD BOUGHT!

The Apostle Paul wrote to the Corinthian church in 1st Corinthians 6:9-11, and I will paraphrase, he said "for us to not be deceived, we all have committed some type of sin in some form or another. First of all we were born in sin as a result of Adam's sinful choice and since have made sinful choices of our own, therefore, we have no room to boast, but because of the name of the Lord, Jesus Christ, we are sanctified and justified all by the Spirit of God." From the book of Genesis to the book of Revelation, God has not only called us, He is calling and using individuals like you and I who were once sinners, to bring deliverance to His people and to proclaim the Gospel of Jesus Christ to the un-churched.

I believe that King David has become one of the most iconic and recognizable men in Bible History today, and he is one of my favorite men to read about. He loved the Lord and he wasn't ashamed to cry out to Him, and God knew his heart and loved him beyond his sinful acts. God revealed to me some truths about myself, He used David's historical testimony of His unfailing Grace and Mercy that He provided for him. He forgave David for his adulterous and murderous acts, and that same Grace and Mercy was given to me when I lost my son and the agony of his loss caused me to lose my natural mind. My fellowship with God was on an emotional roller coaster. I didn't fully understand God's revelation at the time, simply because I didn't feel comfortable with the fact that a Loving, Gracious God would bring up my past life of sin choices, and dangle them before me to get me in a place to accept His will for my life.

However, I understand now, that it wasn't and it isn't God who was remembering my sinful past, it was me who had been keeping it relevant. I relied on my natural sense of "feeling" in response to God's forgiveness. But God shared with me that His forgiveness isn't based on a feeling, but rather on an action that has already been performed. He sent His only begotten Son, Jesus Christ through the birth canal of the Virgin Mary, and He was crucified on the Cross at Calvary. I want to encourage those of you who may be struggle with the guilt of your past or even your present, please be not deceived by the devil any longer, he is always replaying the things that you and I used to do, and his desire is for us to walk in condemnation, but Jesus has come that we may have "life and have that more abundantly" (John 10:10). Regardless of how negative our situation may look, how it may feel or despite how it sounds, God is requiring of us to simply rest in the truth of His word and enjoy this journey called life.

My life as well as the life of David are similar in many ways, based on the truth that both us were chosen by God. David was chosen to be King despite the fact that his own family didn't think he looked the part, and I was chosen before the foundation of the world to be Holy, and I have my doubters and haters as well. Neither of us had the privilege or the right to vote ourselves in or out of God's infinite plan, but along with being chosen by God both of us still made some foolish, sinful mistakes. I didn't say we were fools but the choices we made were to fulfill our natural desires which were not pleasing to the Lord, but because of His love for us, our testimonies are the same, "The righteous cry out, and the Lord hears them; He delivers them from all their troubles." (Psalm 34:17 NIV). David and I didn't mind admitting to God that we had a problem and God didn't despise our brokenness, He took pleasure in providing us with what we needed (Psalm 149:4).

What I love most about the life of David, is the fact that God established a relationship with him that was unbreakable even when he was out of fellowship with Him. And that is how God revealed one of His sacred secrets to me, yes, there were times after losing my son that I made some conscience decisions that caused me to break fellowship with Him, but God's Grace and Mercy would not allow my relationship with Him to be severed, it remained unbreakable, He embraced me with opened arms and refused to allow the devil to have any type of advantage that would cause him to inhabit my eternal life in Him.

My testimony of "Then I Worship" was established through the challenges of going through my final stage of grief; accepting God's Will for my life. God used the story of King David in 2nd Samuel chapter 12, to bring me to a place of understanding His Love for me, but in order to see God's revelation for my life, I had to read and meditate in the book of 2nd Samuel, the eleventh chapter. I needed to know how David himself came to the knowledge of finally realizing that without a doubt, and despite the fact that he had sinned against God and

Heaven, God continued pouring out His Mercy upon him.

Despite the reality of the challenges that I had to endure when I lost my son, God desired for me to come to the realization that He was and is the only one who truly understood how empty my heart was, the loneliness that I felt because of Herman Jr's absence, the depression that I experienced, the sadness that I had to endure because my daughter's heart had been severed because of the loss of her brother, how painful it was for his dad, Herman Sr. to lose his only son and how much grief it brought to our entire family and his friends. God's infinite wisdom guided to me to a place in His word that caused a spiritual awakening in me and it left me with no other choice but to line up with His plan for my life, straighten out my crooked places, turn right and go straight again.

If you have never read or heard any other story in the Holy Bible's history, I'm sure that most of you have heard this one about David in the book of 2nd Samuel chapter eleven. The basic theme of this chapter takes place during King David's reign, the time when the kings of Israel were at war against other nations. King David sent his men out to war but he decided not to go, (the bible doesn't say why he stayed at home), but as the evening was approaching, he went upon his rooftop. There he saw a beautiful woman (Bathsheba) bathing herself, he inquired as to who she was and who's she was (Uriah's wife), he called for her, laid with her and she became pregnant. Her husband (Uriah) returned home from battle. David and Uriah had a small conversation about the status of Joab the commander of David's army, he wanted to know how well he and the soldiers performed while in battle. Then David began his plan of deception of getting Uriah drunk, his desire was for Uriah to become inebriated to the point that he would go home and lay with his own wife, and when her pregnancy was revealed to Uriah, he would think that the child was his. But David's deception didn't work out as he planned, therefore, he sent Uriah back out to war and had him placed or positioned on the front line of fire to assure his death, David's plan prevails and he takes Bathsheba to be his wife.

Now, at the time that God lead me to those particular scriptures, I had some reservation as to why they were important and how significant it was for my life's journey. For quite some time I was convinced and therefore concluded that God was "calling me on the carpet," as he did David when he sent Nathan the prophet to confront him about his adulterous state. I had some skeletons in my closets as well, and the only answer that I could come up with at the time was, that both David and I were being punished because of our sinful actions, and we both lost our sons to death as a result of it.

I struggled with that thought for a period of time and I allowed it to weigh heavy in my mind. So I finally decided that I needed to share my thoughts with someone, and not just anyone, I needed someone to hear and listen to me. I was doing a good job of condemning myself, so I didn't need someone to beat me over the head with the scripture that's found in the book of Galatians 6:7; "do not be deceived, God is not mocked, for whatsoever a man sows that shall he also reap." I'm not allowed to change God's word but I can change how I understand it, the word "whatsoever" can be defined as good, bad or indifferent. It is truly amazing to me that we, yes I'm guilty as well, will only quote that scripture when people have committed sin, fallen short of God's Glory, rarely is it quoted when people are doing that which is right. Now, let's think about it, if the sin seed brings judgement, why can't the righteous seed bring a harvest? JUST A THOUGHT.

I thank God for those who were led by His Spirit to encourage me, and who were courageous enough to tell me the truth; the thoughts that I was having were not of God. He hasn't redeemed me from my sins and then had a change of mind and decided to punish me by taking my son away from me because of my sins. God is the creator and giver of life, He knows our number of days on this earth, death knocked on my son's door at the age of eighteen and that was his time to answer to it, and when I really understood this truth, it helped me to know that if the sins we commit causes someone else to die, then there wouldn't be any human existence on this planet earth, and Jesus' suffering, persecution and crucifixion for our sins would have been and is in vain.

FOOD FOR THOUGHT; God revealed to me is that sometimes we forget to think about the people of "what if", what if the sinner repents to God and is baptized and receives the Holy Spirit, what if they become believers of the death, burial and resurrection of the Lord Jesus Christ, what if God's eyes refuses to see their sins because of the blood of Jesus Christ, what if that person is YOU and I.

Yes, there is not denying, David did lose his son to death because of his sin choices, as recorded in 2nd Samuel chapter 12, God sent Nathan the prophet to reveal such truth to David, but God wanted me to know, that David became a "what if", he knew that after he had been "called on the carpet", he had no other choice but to confess and acknowledge the fact that he had sinned against God, as noted in verse thirteen of chapter twelve, the latter sentence reads, "The Lord also has put away thy sin; thou shalt not die, God could have killed David and his child. Nathan told David that "because of his deed, it gave the enemies of the Lord reason to blaspheme," the enemies of the Lord disrespected Him and judgement came to David's house. His first son that was born to him surely died.

The same MERCY that He provided for David, He had also provided for me and He didn't take my son because of my past sinful acts but because of His Perfect will, it has to be accomplished. It was in my best interest to learn and understand His will, and as a result of that knowledge it would catapult me to the next level of Worship toward Him. I am totally thankful to God for opening up my blinded eyes to see and discern the truth about the lies that the devil was trying to continue to deceive me with. Satan was on a mission to keep me bound and have me walk in condemnation because of my past, he didn't want me to receive God's truth through His word. He would have succeeded if only I had continued accepting the negative thoughts that he was feeding me with and it would have stunted my spiritual growth of searching for the truth of God's word and His plan for my life. I am enormously thankful for the truth of God's love for me, it is genuine and everlasting.

After David's acknowledgement and confession of his sin, he also realized and understood why he lost his son to death. It is one thing for us to confess our sins to God, but the actions that we embark upon after our confession will ultimately determine the path that we walk. God had to cause David to search his heart, it was time for him to take responsibility for his own actions. The events that followed after David's son died, caused an awakening inside of me that was so powerful, all I could say was "For I know that all things work together for the good of those who love the Lord and who are called according to His purpose" (Romans 8:28).

So now, let us examine how David responded to his loss. In 2nd Samuel 12:15-20, I'll paraphrase verses fifteen through nineteen; I will walk you through each step of David's actions as written in verse twenty. When the prophet Nathan left David's house, the Lord struck his child that Uriah's wife had conceived with David, the child became sick. David fasted and prayed to God for the life of his child, despite the fact that David had already been informed that the child would die, it didn't stop him from seeking or bargaining with God for the life of his son. David slept on the ground for seven days, and on that seventh day his child died. His servants were afraid to tell him that his child had died because they feared that he would do himself harm, but when David saw them whispering among themselves, he realized that the child was dead, and he asked them and they replied "he is dead."

This particular story brings tears to my eyes a lot of times when I read it, because as a mother who has lost her son to death, it causes me to replay so many memories of how I searched for answers in God's word that would bring comfort to my son even though he was dead. I know how deeply David's heart was hurting, despite the fact that his son was conceived out of his sinful choices, I believe that David was a man who loved his wife and his son and would have done whatever he could within his power that would cause his son's life to be spared. God created man in His own image to be the head of his home, he is expected to love, provide and protect his family, and when men merely think that they are unable to do those necessary things for their families, some men consider themselves weak, needless, and useless, contrary to how God made them and His thoughts about them.

After David went through his grieving process, God revealed to me some extraordinary wisdom about David's actions, and how it would impact my life in bringing me to a place of understanding His will and purpose for me. Beginning in verse twenty, as recorded in the word of God, "David got up from the ground, he washed and anointed himself, and changed his clothes and came into the House of the Lord and worshiped.'

There are five important things that David did after his son died and finally "Accepted" God's will for his life. Each of the five actions that David embarked upon were connected by the word "and", it is used four times in verse twenty; the word "and" has a positive connection that has become a valuable, trustworthy cause for me while I was study and meditating upon God's word. It is a "conjunction word that is used to connect things together, to demonstrate a continual action of something being done." After all of the challenges and pain that David and I had to suffer through when we lost our sons, God's will had to be done, I understand now that God had to put me in the right position to really hear from Him. There were necessary steps that I had to take, in order to get in a place to totally surrender my will to His will and allow it to be done. I had to see myself for who I really was and realize that He is in control of my entire being. "In Him I move, live and have my being" (Acts 17:28 KJV).

When David was lying upon the earth, it became the perfect place for him to exemplify humility. In the book of 1st Peter 5:6 NIV, we should do as written, "Humble yourselves, therefore, under God's mighty hand, that he may lift you up in due time." God wanted me to know that just as David had to throw himself to the ground and cry out to Him for help, I had to relinquish my will and my entire being unto Him, the best way for me to go up was to go down. Humility isn't a sign of weakness but an indicator of strength. During Jesus' earthly ministry, he told His disciples that "the greatest one in the kingdom of heaven would be the one who humbles himself as a little child." I had to learn how to surpass my thoughts of "woe is me" and allow God to elevate my mind and my spirit up to where it belonged. One of my life's lesson is to decrease in my flesh and allow God to increase in my spirit.

The next action that David performed was getting up from the ground or the earth, he could no longer lay upon the earth in his misery, he realized that the Lord wasn't going to change His mind and restore his son's life; (although He could have), but God can't and will not lie. David was still the chosen King of Israel who had responsibilities, there were still military men who were under his command that looked to him for instructions, and he had a wife (Bathsheba), whom he had to provide for, protect, love and care for.

A very valuable lesson and a sure truth about life is, it

doesn't cease from happening because we lose our relationship with other people, whether it is because of divorce of a marriage, di-vision of friendship or even when we lose someone because of death, regardless of how severe the pain is as a result of our loss, we must remember that if God allows us to see another Graced-filled day, it will be another day of not having that individual here with us. For quite some time that statement didn't set to well in my spirit and it felt like the reality of my son's death was diminished, but the truth was that it was imperative for me to make a conscious decision to accept that there is no life in the grave and if God "WILLED IT", He has a plan that is greater than mine. And if I continued to live in the pain of my loss it would eventually cause me to forget and take for granted that God had blessed our family with Herman Jr. for eighteen years, years that some families could only wish for. It was God who Blessed my husband and I with ability to conceive our son and He fortified my womb to be able carry him to full term and give birth to him, we had eighteen years with him, no more, no less, that was in God's Master Plan from the beginning, therefore, I simply have to trust in His Perfect Will.

David found strength after getting up from the ground, and the bible states "he washed and anointed himself," he washed himself for the cleansing purposes for his natural body, seven days of lying on the ground presents a need to cleanse; and he anointed himself with oil as a symbol for re-dedicating himself back unto the Lord. I'm sure David had cried many tears and prayed without ceasing for the Lord to spare his son's life, but to no avail. I believe that God strategically inspired Samuel to pen the statement about the anointing and washing of David's body. When you think about water and how refreshing it is when we wash or bathe ourselves, there is something about water that has some significant characteristics. It is strong enough to destroy an entire city but gentle enough to refresh our natural body, rejuvenate our soul, mind, and regenerate our physical body. There was no way that David could have washed away the truth of the agony and pain that he had to endure when he lost his son, but I believe that he knew without a shadow of doubt that the Lord loved him enough to sustain him through his pain. After he refreshed himself naturally it prepared him for the next phase in his life, a Life of Worship, allowing God's Will to fortify him.

After David's servants informed him that his son was dead, the bible stated the he "changed his apparel", for seven days David laid upon the earth in what was called sackcloth apparel, according to Wikipedia's encyclopedia, the texture was "coarse, usually made out of goat's hair," sackcloth was worn and used in the Old Testament as a sign or mourning and or repentance. As he wallowed or laid upon the earth, it must have been an uncomfortable ordeal for him, but it was no match to David's injured heart.

David eventually accepted the truth about his son's death, and the time came for him to rise up and change out of his current wardrobe, which consisted of the earth's dirt, his tears of sorrow, pain, and mourning, it was time for the Lord to robe him with a GARMENT of Praise. This turn of events in David's life caused my heart to be more receptive to what God was trying to convey to me, and in order for me to excel into the next level of change in Him, I had to exchange my spirit of heaviness that had clothed my mind with negative thoughts and put on His spiritual garment of PRAISE, knowledge and understanding.

God opened up my understanding through His word that is written in Isaiah 61:3 KJV, God had already set His precedence of comfort for "those who mourned in Zion," my revelation is that He has given me "beauty for ashes, the oil of joy for my mourning, the GARMENT of Praise, for my spirit of heaviness. I know now that God himself "knows the plans he has for me, plans to prosper me and not to harm me, plans to give me hope and a future," (Jeremiah 29:11 NIV). David and I had no other choice but to cast away our old robe of mourning and accept God's New Robe of Righteous.

After David changed his wardrobe, "he went into the house of the Lord and worshipped." The more I read this story of David, I often wondered why and how did David go from a state of mourning, laying upon the ground for seven days, fasting, refusing to eat or drink, praying to God for deliverance of his son's life, and in a matter of a few days end up in the House of the Lord in a posture of Worship?

Well, the conclusion of the matter is that God is so amazing and He has an awesome way of revealing truths to us when we need it the most. He answered that question for me so that I can share it with you, the answers will not be found in the how's and why's but rather, it is in WHOM. When everything else fails and everyone has gone on with life as usual, God was and is the one who has been and is my very present help in my time of need, He promised to never leave me nor forsake me, He is my strong tower that I can run into and feel safe, my burden bearer and heavy load carrier, The God in whom I can trust.

During the times when I was at my lowest level of mental and physical struggles, my bout with depression, oppression, my heart ached so deep within, I literally spent many days and nights prostrate on my bedroom floor, crying to God out of an earnest heart for Him to just give me strength to go on with life. There were so many times that I didn't know what to pray for or how to pray, I could only weep, days that I cried so hard my eyelids would swell and my head would ache from the pressure of my agony. But God! I am so grateful to Him for hearing my cry and for keeping me wrapped up in His loving arms. He was the only one who truly understood what I was going through, regardless of how long it took for me to accept the truth of His will, God loved me through my pain, He didn't cast me away from His presence but rather, He hid me under the shadow of His wings. And for this cause I'm able to share with you the truth of His Mercy. Many times when I chose to act contrary to His word, He allowed Mercy to grant me another chance, and another chance and another chance, and He lead me to a place and a position of "Then I Worship".

The word then is an adverb that has several meanings and the one that I can relate to the most, is found in Merriam-Webster's dictionary, "soon after that, next in order of". When it was all said and done and the dust begin to settle after losing my son, I looked back over my life and examined it, I took inventory of how I responded to each stage of my grief and it wasn't a pretty site, but the beauty that I saw was God's handiwork from the beginning until this present day. He knew and orchestrated every event that took place in my life so very precisely. He was ever present, my very help in time of need. Because of His Love for me, I have no other choice but to say, despite all that I've had to go through, God ordained my struggles and my challenges to cause me to have a life of "Then I Worship".

Just as David relied/depended on God to be his very strength, I had to take note of his testimony, David couldn't stay in that same state of agony and defeat, he had to get up and do something about it; "faith without works is dead" (James 2:17KJV), he had to change his negative, present situation in order to have a positive outcome. He knew without a shadow of doubt of his past experience of victories were as a result of the Lord's Faithfulness toward him, he was chosen as king after God's own heart. David had no other choice but to go to the one who was responsible for his very being, and as a result he had to go into the Lord's House and Worship.

The word of God tells us that "God is spirit, and His worshippers must worship in the Spirit and in truth" (John 4:24 KJV). Anybody can praise God, but not everybody can worship God, worship isn't about the location or physicality; a song that is being sung and heard under the anointing will give cause for all of us to praise God, but when we are in the lowest of lows, and our pain is fierce, it is our "attitude that will determine our altitude", worship is factored in when we reverence Him out of a pure, honest heart as The God of Deity and regardless of what may be going on in our lives, our worship to God should be a virtuous attribute that we can hang our hats on!!!

I believe that nothing happens by chance, all things work together; whether it is good, bad or indifferent, and a true worshipper knows how to BLESS God and PRESS through any and all obstacles. Victory can be achieved through one battle, but to be Victorious, you will have a testimony that says, despite the storms, the wind and the rains, it is God who has caused you to be Triumphant!!! I want to admonish you, the people of the Most High God, there is a Worshipper in you, and God is patiently waiting for you to surrender. It's not a difficult request, however, we make it challenging at times, but it is not impossible.

I understand and accept God's will for my life now more than ever before, and I am so very Thankful for Him. The path that He chose for me to walk in, is leading me to a more grandeur destination, than the one I had for myself. So, I therefore, choose to trust and love Him with all of my heart, mind, and strength. The length of time that I spent mourning the loss of my son was greater than the number of days that David endured, but regardless of the time, I've learned that time only exists in its natural habitat but God, who is eternal, has established the end result of a matter before the beginning. After all I had to endure, it brought to my position of "Then I Worship."

When something is sure to happen, such as death, and you are on the life side of it, it will alter your very state of being but it won't define who you are as a born again believer of Jesus Christ. So be encouraged my friend, this is not the time or the place to throw in the towel, because there is still HOPE, the songwriter sings, "My Hope is built upon nothing less, than Jesus' Blood and His Righteousness". Nothing catches God by surprise, He knows every tear that you will cry, every heart that aches, and every question that begins with "WHY." God is your very present help in time of need. The path that God has ordained for you will become your obstacle course, but please remember, when God orders it and He will, He has enough confidence in you and will give you every TRUTH of His Word that will cause you to navigate through it and you will have your own Testimony of "Then I Worship." Then you will be in a position to pay it forward to someone else, this law of reciprocity is a WIN-WIN!!! I love you with the Lord of the Lord and there is nothing you can do about it, keep your head up in a Posture of Worship!!!

MY MOTTO

The Lord is my Shepherd; I shall not want.

He makes me to lie down in green pastures;

He leads me beside the still waters.

He restores my soul; He leads me in the path of
righteousness for His name's sake.

Yea, though I walk through the valley of the shadow
of death, I will fear no evil; for you are with me;

Your rod and your staff, they comfort me.

You prepare a table before me in the presence of my
enemies;

You anoint my head with oil; my cup runs over.

Surely goodness and mercy shall follow me all the
days of my life;

And I will dwell in the House of the Lord Forever.

THE LEGACY LIVES ON

When will I be missing you?
When my kids ask for their uncle Herman, I'll be missing you.
When Brooklynn says "I wish my daddy was here", I'll be missing you.
When Jeremy says "Tip what is my brother up to"? I'll be missing you.
When my husband needs the grass cut, I'll be missing you.
When my mom cries at night, I'll be missing you.
When my dad says "Man take care of yourself and stay out of trouble, I'll be missing you.
When I need someone to talk to, I'll be missing you.
When the students at Spain Park don't see you in the hallway, I'll be missing you.
When skies are gray and oh! So blue, I'll be missing you.
When the seasons change from summer to fall, I'll be missing you.
When it's February 21st, I'll be missing you.
When I long to see your smiling face, I'll be missing you.
When I long to hear you call out to me "Tip I need you to do something for me". I'll be missing you.
I will be forever...Missing you
Your sister "Tip"
In Loving memory of her brother
Herman Hunter, Jr. (AKA "P")

SYNOPSIS OF "THEN I WORSHIP"

Then I Worship has been written for you and to every individual on this great planet earth, to use as a spiritual and powerful tool, to help encourage and inspire you to stand in your own truth of the pain and suffering that will accompany you when you lose a loved one or a friend/confidant to death. I will assure you that God is well aware of your pain and He has declared in His Holy Word, "That He will never leave you nor forsake you" (Hebrews 13:5). My prayer is that each individual will recover in and with love, unity and strength, and realize that those of us who die in that Blessed Hope-Jesus Christ... are on a stepping stone to get to our God-Given Destiny.

ABOUT THE AUTHOR

Janice Neeley was born and raised in Alabaster, Alabama by some of the most loving and powerful women of God. Being raised without her father's presence was life changing but not life altering. Her spiritual journey was birth before the foundation of the world, and before the manifestation of her new birth, life happened and she made some unwise choices that took her to some unpleasant places in locality and in her natural mind. But God, who knew her then and He knows her now, He has raised her up to be a conduit for The Gospel of Jesus Christ, and has given her a ministry of servitude for those in need.

She is an active member in her local church assembly/New Wineskins Ministries International, under the leadership of Pastor Donald R. Bivins Jr. and Pastor Dionne Bivins, they have been called by God and continue to be faithful and loyal to their call. Our church Moto is for everyone to receive a fresh touch and a fresh taste of the New Wine of Jesus Christ as noted in the book of Matthew 9:17 KJV, "Nor do they put new wine into old wineskins, or else the wineskins break, the wine is spilled, and the wineskins are ruined. But they put new wine into new wineskins, and both are preserved."

www.ingramcontent.com/pod-product-compliance
Lightning Source LLC
Chambersburg PA
CBHW051707090426
42736CB00013B/2580